The Official
Arsenal
Annual 2010

Written by Chas Newkey-Burden

A Grange Publication

© 2009. Published by Grange Communications Ltd., Edinburgh, under licence from Arsenal Football Club. Printed in the EU.

ISBN 978-1-906211-71-4

£6.99

CONTENTS

Dear Supporters,

I wish you a very warm welcome to The Official Arsenal Annual 2010.

The 2008/09 season was an exciting and promising one for the Club. Although we were disappointed to not win a trophy, we could take many positives from the campaign. We reached the semi-finals of two competitions – the Champions League and FA Cup – and qualified for Europe once more. In the final 23 games of the season we only lost one match at the Emirates. I feel the squad is moving forward all the time.

There were so many memorable matches. The 5-2 defeat of Fenerbahce in Turkey, the victories over Manchester United and Chelsea in the Premier League, the 6-0 defeat of Sheffield United in the Carling Cup and the 4-4 draws with Tottenham Hotspur and Liverpool among them. The players fought on four fronts and made me very proud.

Everyone at the Club has been looking forward to the 2009/10 season and I am sure we can improve on last season's form. We have a very solid, committed and skilful set of players who are capable of competing with the best of England and Europe.

Arsenal is a very special Club and I am honoured to be the manager. You, the supporters, are a big part of what makes this Club special. I am always grateful and moved by your loyal and vocal support. Along with the players I thank you for your backing and look forward to an exciting season ahead.

With thanks,

Arsène Wenger
Manager

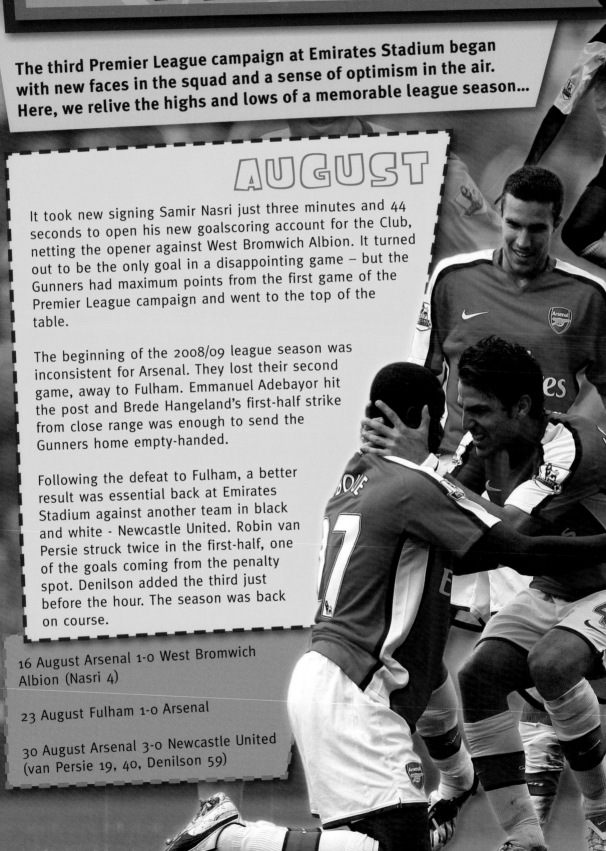

The third Premier League campaign at Emirates Stadium began with new faces in the squad and a sense of optimism in the air. Here, we relive the highs and lows of a memorable league season...

AUGUST

It took new signing Samir Nasri just three minutes and 44 seconds to open his new goalscoring account for the Club, netting the opener against West Bromwich Albion. It turned out to be the only goal in a disappointing game – but the Gunners had maximum points from the first game of the Premier League campaign and went to the top of the table.

The beginning of the 2008/09 league season was inconsistent for Arsenal. They lost their second game, away to Fulham. Emmanuel Adebayor hit the post and Brede Hangeland's first-half strike from close range was enough to send the Gunners home empty-handed.

Following the defeat to Fulham, a better result was essential back at Emirates Stadium against another team in black and white - Newcastle United. Robin van Persie struck twice in the first-half, one of the goals coming from the penalty spot. Denilson added the third just before the hour. The season was back on course.

16 August Arsenal 1-0 West Bromwich Albion (Nasri 4)

23 August Fulham 1-0 Arsenal

30 August Arsenal 3-0 Newcastle United (van Persie 19, 40, Denilson 59)

SEPTEMBER

In the eighth minute at Ewood Park, Theo Walcott set up Van Persie to stab home the opening goal. However, the match was really all about Emmanuel Adebayor. The Togan netted a fine hat-trick, which he completed in injury time. Also notable was the substitute appearance of Jack Wilshere, who became the youngest player to appear in a league game for the Club at just 16 years 256 days.

Another trip north and another win for the Gunners came at Bolton Wanderers seven days later. Having gone behind after 14 minutes, goals from Eboue, Bendtner and Denilson sealed the points for the visitors. Eboue's strike was the first Premier League goal of his career and the match was also memorable for some fine goalkeeping from Manuel Almunia.

Cesc Fabregas was key to the opening goal against Hull City back at Emirates Stadium, but the visitors' Paul McShane was credited with the final touch. With that own goal separating the teams, two goals in four second-half minutes gave Hull City a surprise victory. Once more, it had been a mixed month for Arsenal.

13 September
Blackburn Rovers 0-4
Arsenal (Van Persie
9, Adebayor 45, 78
(pen), 89)

20 September Bolton
Wanderers 1-3 Arsenal
(Eboue 26, Bendtner
27, Denilson 87)

27 September Arsenal
1-2 Hull City
(McShane 42, og)

SEASON REPORT
PREMIER LEAGUE

OCTOBER

October began and ended with a draw. Sandwiched in between were two victories. However, that description barely does justice to a truly dramatic month in the league.

At Sunderland, the Gunners seemed sure to be staring defeat in the face when they went behind in the 85th minute. However, the closing minutes of the tie were high-octane as the visitors piled forward. Eventually the pressure told and Fabregas levelled the scoreline in stoppage time.

Having fallen behind in the ninth minute, Arsenal fought back in a great second-half against Everton at Emirates Stadium. Substitute Walcott ignited the team and sealed the afternoon with his 90th minute strike. The Gunners might have been inconsistent, but they were showing consistent ability to fight back.

Adebayor followed Fabregas with a 90th minute goal at West Ham United, which doubled the lead for the visitors after an own goal 15 minutes earlier. Two wins on the spin was the perfect preparation for the north London derby three days later. Tottenham had a new manager in Harry Redknapp - could the Gunners spoil his debut?

Nearly, was the answer. With just two minutes remaining of the tie, Arsenal were 4-2 ahead and the fans were jubilantly celebrating an expected victory thanks to goals from Silvestre, Gallas, Adebayor and Van Persie. Then, Spurs struck twice in two minutes through Jermaine Jena and Aaron Lennon, grabbing a dramatic draw.

4 October Sunderland 1-1 Arsenal (Fabregas 90)

18 October Arsenal 3-1 Everton
(Nasri 48, Van Persie 70, Walcott 90)

26 October West Ham 0-2 Arsenal
(Faubert 75 (og), Adebayor 90)

29 October Arsenal 4-4 Tottenham Hotspur
(Silvestre 37, Gallas 46, Adebayor 64, Van Persie 68)

NOVEMBER

In November, the Gunners had two great victories over the teams they would expect to compete with for the Premier League top spot but lost their three other games.

Gael Clichy scored his first league goal of the season at Stoke City but his 90th minute long-range strike could not save Wenger's team from defeat after the home side had already struck twice.

Back at home, Manchester United were the next opponents. The game began in heavy rain but by the end the sun was shining and the Arsenal fans were smiling. Two goals from Nasri gave them the points and suddenly the Gunners were looking on good form again. Could they take this result and go on a run of wins?

Not against Aston Villa they couldn't. This time Clichy scored at the wrong end and Agbonlahor doubled the visitors' lead 11 minutes later. They were to lose at Manchester City, too. Three second-half goals at Eastlands condemned the Gunners to their second loss on the spin.

Had the Gunners lost their next match at Chelsea they would have been left 13 points behind the league leaders. A Johan Djourou own goal put them behind and a third successive defeat looked on the cards. However, two goals in 120 seconds from Van Persie gave the Gunners not just victory but renewed confidence.

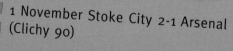

1 November Stoke City 2-1 Arsenal
(Clichy 90)

8 November Arsenal 2-1 Manchester United
(Nasri 22, 48)

15 November Arsenal 0-2 Aston Villa

22 November Manchester City 3-0 Arsenal

30 November Chelsea 1-2 Arsenal
(Van Persie 60, 62)

DECEMBER

After two defeats in November, the Gunners were unbeaten during December. Instead they picked up two wins and three draws – not ideal but a step in the right direction.

Adebayor scored the only goal of the game against Wigan Athletic in the 16th minute but there could easily have been a much bigger scoreline. The Gunners hit the woodwork several times and Almunia made some inspired saves at the other end.

The Togan was again on target at Middlesbrough the following week, nodding home Fabregas's corner in the 17th minute. However, a former Gunner was about to twist the plot. Jeremie Aliadiere headed an equaliser 12 minutes later and the scoreline remained 1-1 until the final whistle.

It was the Merseysiders who were their next opponents. Van Persie put Arsenal ahead in the first-half but Robbie Keane levelled the scoreline just before the break. The Gunners were unable to break ahead in the second-half and their task was not eased by the dismissal of Adebayor for two yellow cards. Wenger's team then drew 2-2 at Aston Villa, with Diaby and Denilson on-target.

A fourth successive draw would have been a disappointing way to end 2008. With just nine minutes to go against Portsmouth, Gallas ensured that would not be the case. He beat David James to the ball and nodded the winner of a tough encounter. Could this win be a springboard to an improved second-half of the Premier League campaign?

6 December Arsenal 1-0 Wigan Athletic (Adebayor 16)

13 December Middlesbrough 1-1 Arsenal (Adebayor 17)

21 December Arsenal 1-1 Liverpool (Van Persie 25)

26 December Aston Villa 2-2 Arsenal (Denilson 40, Diaby 48)

28 December Arsenal 1-0 Portsmouth (Gallas 81)

SEASON REPORT
PREMIER LEAGUE

JANUARY

In the first match of 2009, Wenger's team found Bolton Wanderers to be formidable opponents. Arsenal attacked, attacked and attacked but it seemed the deadlock would not be broken. Then with six minutes left, substitute Bendtner grabbed the winner with a sliding shot.

The Gunners travelled to Hull City determined to avenge the September defeat – and they did. In the last seven minutes Nasri and in-form Bendtner struck to complete a 3-1 scoreline. The Dane almost added a fourth in injury time.

Another game, another late goal: this time Everton were the opponents. Tim Cahill had given the home side the lead just after the hour, and it took until injury time for the Gunners to give their reply. With seconds remaining, Van Persie unleashed a potent shot which levelled the scoreline.

Arsenal dominated their home match against West Ham United, with Diaby and Adebayor both coming close to breaking the deadlock. It never was broken, however, and the Gunners ended January with another draw. Would they turn draws into victories in February...

10 January Arsenal 1-0 Bolton Wanderers
(Bendtner 84)

17 January Hull City 1-3 Arsenal
(Adebayor 30, Nasri 83, Bendtner 86)

28 January Everton 1-1 Arsenal
(Van Persie 90)

31 January Arsenal 0-0 West Ham United

FEBRUARY

They would not and neither would they score. However, at least they did not lose – with all three league ties concluding as goalless draws.

Away to Tottenham Hotspur a draw was impressive after three mad first-half minutes deprived the Gunners of the services of Adebayor (injury) and Eboue (red card). Alexandre Song and Bendtner both came close to scoring, but in the circumstances a draw was an admirable result.

New signing Andrey Arshavin was impressive against Sunderland back at Emirates Stadium. However, even the Russian's brilliance could not break the deadlock and another game ended in a goalless draw. The closest the Gunners came to scoring was when Kolo Toure's effort was cleared off the line.

The frustration of all Arsenal fans was clear when the team registered their fourth successive goalless draw with a 0-0 finish against Fulham. Van Persie came closest to scoring but was denied by Mark Schwarzer. Despite the disappointment that the Gunners had not won, this was their 15th game unbeaten.

8 February Tottenham Hotspur 0-0 Arsenal

21 February Arsenal 0-0 Sunderland

28 February Arsenal 0-0 Fulham

SEASON REPORT
PREMIER LEAGUE

MARCH

The Gunners remained unbeaten in the league during March but went one better than that – they won all three league ties in style!

The long goal drought ended at the Hawthorns in the Spring. All three Arsenal goals came in the first half: two from Bendtner, one from Toure. The pick of the Dane's two strikes was his 44th minute volley. The three points were welcome, as was the end of 364 excruciating minutes without a goal. The goals came thick and fast against Blackburn Rovers, with Arshavin scoring his first for Arsenal from an impossibly tight angle. Eboue then scored twice in the final two minutes, once from the penalty spot, to complete a 4-0 victory. The Gunners were back on form!

They remained on form at Newcastle United seven days later. Second-half goals from Bendtner, Diaby and Nasri saw the Gunners sail to a thoroughly deserved victory. Almunia, too, was key in the win. The Spaniard saved a first-half penalty from Obafemi Martins.

3 March West Bromwich Albion 1-3 Arsenal
(Bendtner 4, 44, Toure 38)

14 March Arsenal 4-0 Blackburn Rovers
(Ooijer 2 (og), Arshavin 65, Eboue 88, 90 (pen))

21 March Newcastle United 1-3 Arsenal
(Bendtner 57, Diaby 63, Nasri 66)

APRIL

The goalless run seemed a distant memory as the team scored 12 goals in just four league games during April. The Gunners were firing once more!

Against Manchester City, Fabregas and Walcott returned from injury following a combined absence of nearly four months. Both were impressive but it was Adebayor who scored both the goals that secured victory.

Away to Wigan, the Gunners were magnificent. Hossam Mido gave the host a first-half lead but the second-half was witness to a stirring comeback. After Walcott equalised on the hour, Silvestre put the visitors ahead in his first game for three months. Arshavin and Song made it four at the death.

The Russian striker was the only Arsenal player to score at Anfield a week later – but he did manage to do it four times. Astonishing, but even more astonishing is that those goals were not enough to win the match. The Gunners were on the brink of a 4-3 win when Yossi Benayoun snatched a late equaliser to level the score. A very dramatic evening at Anfield had been had.

Prior to the match at Middlesbrough, Fabregas had just one goal to his name during an injury-disrupted campaign. He scored twice against the north-easterners thanks to assists from Arshavin and Eboue. The Gunners were closing in on a fourth-placed finish and a Champions League qualification place for the following campaign. The team had not lost in the league for 20 games and had not conceded a league goal at home since December 21.

4 April Arsenal 2-0 Manchester City
(Adebayor 8, 49)

11 April Wigan Athletic 1-4 Arsenal
(Walcott 60, Silvestre 71, Arshavin 90, Song 90)

21 April Liverpool 4-4 Arsenal
(Arshavin 36, 67, 70, 90)

26 April Arsenal 2-0 Middlesbrough
(Fabregas 26, 67)

SEASON REPORT
PREMIER LEAGUE

MAY

Fourth place was secured in May and with it Champions League qualification for 2009/10.

Great Dane Bendtner netted a brace against Portsmouth, with Carlos Vela adding a third in the second period. In truth, the Gunners had been in control of the match throughout and could have had many more goals.

Chelsea were the penultimate league visitors to Emirates Stadium and they inflicted the heaviest defeat the stadium had seen to date. Bendtner headed home on 70 minutes, but by full-time Arsenal were losing 4-1.

And so to Old Trafford, where Manchester United needed just a draw with the Gunners to win the Premier League. It is to Arsenal's credit that they held United to a 0-0 draw. Indeed, coming close through Van Persie and Fabregas, the visitors could easily have won.

The season closed with a home tie against Stoke City. Van Persie was on fire and was involved in all of Arsenal's goals. He set up two and scored two as the Gunners put in a rampant performance that boded well for the following campaign.

2 May Portsmouth 0-3 Arsenal
(Bendtner 13, 40, Vela 56)

10 May Arsenal 1-4 Chelsea (Bendtner 70)

16 May Manchester United 0-0 Arsenal

24 May Arsenal 4-1 Stoke City
(Beattie 10 (og), Van Persie 16 (pen), 41, Diaby 18)

POSITIONAL SENSE

All Arsenal fans dream of pulling on the red and white shirt and playing for this brilliant Club. But do you know which position you would play in? Are you sure? Take this fun quiz and find out which is the best one for you: defence, midfield or upfront!

When you watch football, do you cheer loudest at:

a) A good solid tackle

b) An exquisite pass

c) A goal that bulges the back of the net

If you see a loose ball during a kick-about is your first thought:

a) I must snuff out the danger

b) Who can I pass this too?

c) It's worth a dig!

Do you prefer to do most of your business in:

a) Your own box

b) From box to box

c) In their box

Which of the following statements do you think most describes you?

a) I am fearless and I like to mark

b) I am fearless and I like to pass

c) I am fearless and don't even try to mark me!

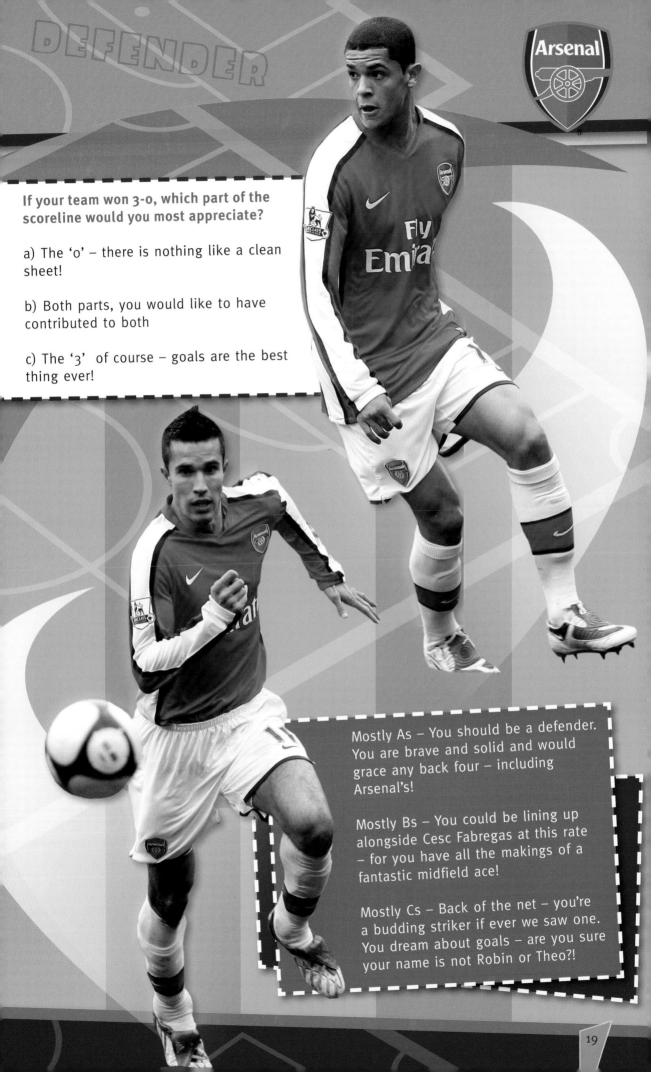

If your team won 3-0, which part of the scoreline would you most appreciate?

a) The '0' – there is nothing like a clean sheet!

b) Both parts, you would like to have contributed to both

c) The '3' of course – goals are the best thing ever!

Mostly As – You should be a defender. You are brave and solid and would grace any back four – including Arsenal's!

Mostly Bs – You could be lining up alongside Cesc Fabregas at this rate – for you have all the makings of a fantastic midfield ace!

Mostly Cs – Back of the net – you're a budding striker if ever we saw one. You dream about goals – are you sure your name is not Robin or Theo?!

QUALIFYING ROUND

FC Twente v Arsenal

Arsenal faced former England manager Steve McClaren's side FC Twente. Wenger's team were up against enormous pressure from the home side in the first-half but came into their own after the break. William Gallas broke the deadlock in the 63rd minute and eight minutes from time Emmanuel Adebayor doubled the lead to give the Gunners a comfortable buffer going into the home leg at Emirates Stadium. A good start for the Gunners.

Euro fact: This was the third time Arsenal have been in the qualifying stages, the third time they have been drawn away first and the third time they have won 2-0.

Arsenal v FC Twente

Despite a comfortable lead, the Gunners were in no mood to play it safe in the second-leg. Instead they took the game to the visitors and won 4-0, making it a thumping 6-0 aggregate victory. After Samir Nasri opened the scoring with a fine solo effort in the first-half, Gallas, Theo Walcott and Nicklas Bendtner tied up the scoring in the second period. Watch out Europe!

Euro fact: This was Nasri's first European goal in an Arsenal shirt.

13 August 2008 FC Twente 0-2 Arsenal
(Gallas 63, Adebayor 83)

27 August 2008 Arsenal 4-0 FC Twente
(Nasri 27, Gallas 52, Walcott 66, Bendtner 89)

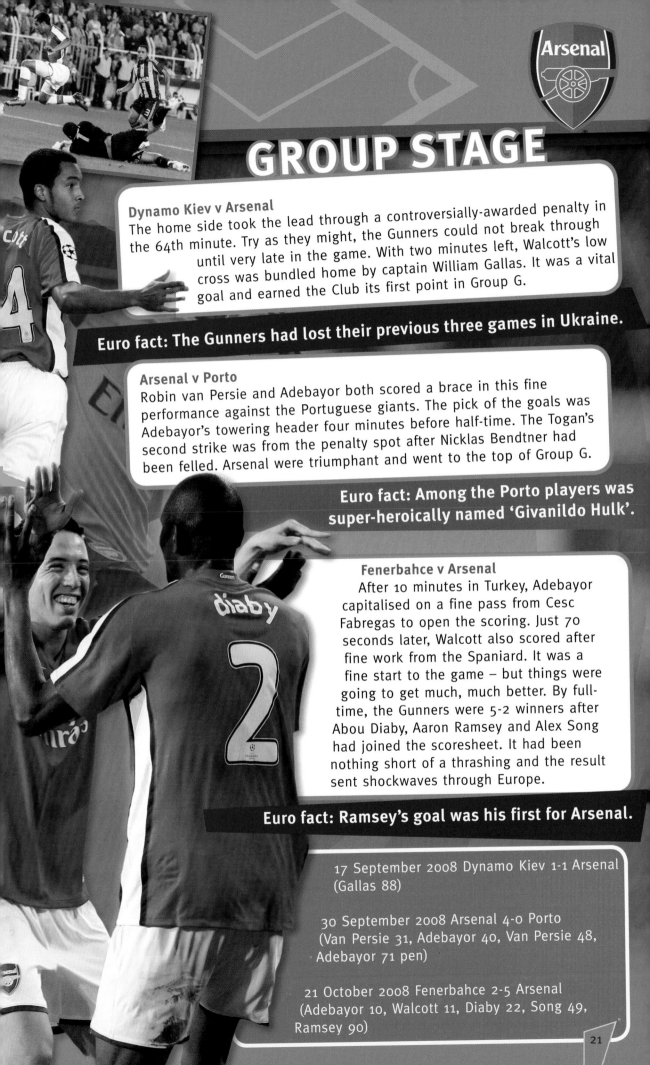

GROUP STAGE

Dynamo Kiev v Arsenal

The home side took the lead through a controversially-awarded penalty in the 64th minute. Try as they might, the Gunners could not break through until very late in the game. With two minutes left, Walcott's low cross was bundled home by captain William Gallas. It was a vital goal and earned the Club its first point in Group G.

Euro fact: The Gunners had lost their previous three games in Ukraine.

Arsenal v Porto

Robin van Persie and Adebayor both scored a brace in this fine performance against the Portuguese giants. The pick of the goals was Adebayor's towering header four minutes before half-time. The Togan's second strike was from the penalty spot after Nicklas Bendtner had been felled. Arsenal were triumphant and went to the top of Group G.

Euro fact: Among the Porto players was super-heroically named 'Givanildo Hulk'.

Fenerbahce v Arsenal

After 10 minutes in Turkey, Adebayor capitalised on a fine pass from Cesc Fabregas to open the scoring. Just 70 seconds later, Walcott also scored after fine work from the Spaniard. It was a fine start to the game – but things were going to get much, much better. By full-time, the Gunners were 5-2 winners after Abou Diaby, Aaron Ramsey and Alex Song had joined the scoresheet. It had been nothing short of a thrashing and the result sent shockwaves through Europe.

Euro fact: Ramsey's goal was his first for Arsenal.

17 September 2008 Dynamo Kiev 1-1 Arsenal
(Gallas 88)

30 September 2008 Arsenal 4-0 Porto
(Van Persie 31, Adebayor 40, Van Persie 48,
Adebayor 71 pen)

21 October 2008 Fenerbahce 2-5 Arsenal
(Adebayor 10, Walcott 11, Diaby 22, Song 49,
Ramsey 90)

GROUP STAGE

Arsenal v Fenerbahce
Despite the goalless scoreline, this tie could easily have finished with another goal-fest because the Gunners were far from shy. Van Persie in particular had several chances and even hit the bar shortly before half-time. In the second-half Diaby came close with a header from a free-kick as the home side continued to attack in numbers. However, the game was to end all-square.

Euro fact: Among the many injured before this game were Theo Walcott, Emmanuel Adebayor, Manuel Almunia and William Gallas.

Arsenal v FC Dynamo Kiev
In his first match as Arsenal captain, Fabregas was again a key figure in a Gunners triumph. After a fine first-half performance from Wenger's team, the home side seemed to fade towards the end of the tie. However, with just four minutes left the Spaniard sent a long pass forward which was to transform the evening and send the Gunners through to the knockout stage. The pass was controlled by Bendtner and the Dane thumped the ball home.

Euro fact: Substitute Jack Wilshere became Arsenal's youngest ever European player at 16 years 329 days.

Porto v Arsenal
Both sides were already guaranteed a place in the knockout stage prior to kick-off. This match therefore became a fight for first place in Group G. The Gunners had to settle for second place after goals either side of the half-time break consigned them to a 2-0 defeat. The visitors rarely threatened to score, with a Bendtner free-kick coming closest. Still, they were through to the knockout stage.

Euro fact: This was Arsène Wenger's 700th game in charge of Arsenal.

5 November 2008 Arsenal 0-0 Fenerbahce

25 November 2008 Arsenal 1-0 Dynamo Kiev (Bendtner 87)

10 December 2008 Porto 2-0 Arsenal

	P	W	D	L	F	A	Pts
1. FC Porto	6	4	0	2	9	8	12
2. Arsenal	6	3	2	1	11	5	11
3. FC Dynamo Kiev	6	2	2	2	4	4	8
4. Fenerbahce	6	0	2	4	4	11	2

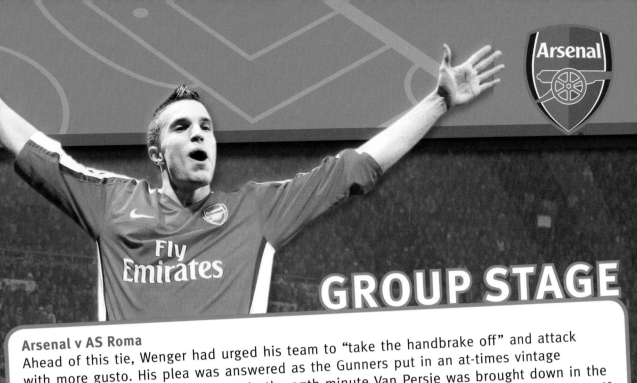

GROUP STAGE

Arsenal v AS Roma

Ahead of this tie, Wenger had urged his team to "take the handbrake off" and attack with more gusto. His plea was answered as the Gunners put in an at-times vintage performance with attacks aplenty. In the 37th minute Van Persie was brought down in the box during one such surge forward. The Dutchman converted the resultant penalty himself confidently. Diaby, Bendtner and Nasri all came close to adding to the scoreline but the tie ended 1-0, a lead for Arsenal to take to Italy for the second-leg.

Euro fact: This was the Gunners' 23rd successive unbeaten tie in Europe.

AS Roma v Arsenal

Juan's 10th minute strike cancelled out the Gunners lead from the first leg. Both sides then scrambled to take the lead. A Gael Clichy cross was nearly converted by Diaby and Toure and Sagna also came close. However, the tie went to a penalty shoot-out and after Almunia's save cancelled out Eduardo's miss, victory was Arsenal's when Max Tonetto blazed his spot-kick over the bar. The Gunners were through to the quarter-finals!

Euro fact: The AS Roma line-up included former Arsenal star Julio Baptista.

24 February 2009 Arsenal 1-0 Roma (Van Persie 37 pen)

11 March 2009 Roma 1-0 Arsenal (Arsenal won 7-6 on penalties)

SEASON REPORT
CHAMPIONS LEAGUE

QUARTER-FINALS

Villarreal v Arsenal

When the home side went into the break 1-0 ahead it was a thoroughly deserved lead after a poor first-half performance from the Gunners. However, the second period was an entirely different story as Arsenal took control of the game and attacked in style. In the 66th minute, Adebayor chested down a pass from Fabregas and scored with a delicious overhead shot that sailed into the far corner. Honours were even on the night and going into the second-leg.

Euro Fact: Former Gunner Robert Pires was in the opposition line-up.

Arsenal v Villarreal

The Gunners sailed into the Champions League semi-final with a magnificent performance against the Spanish. Wenger's men were in an imperious mood and in the 10th minute, Walcott fired home past Diego Lopez to give Arsenal the lead. Adebayor steered home a second on the hour and the Gunners had a precious cushion between them and the Spaniards. Nine minutes later Walcott was fouled in the area and Van Persie converted from the penalty spot.

Euro Fact: This was only the second time that Arsenal had qualified for the semi-finals.

7 April 2009 Villarreal 1-1 Arsenal
(Adebayor 66)

15 April 2009 Arsenal 3-0 Villarreal
(Walcott 10, Adebayor 60, Van Persie 69 pen)

SEMI-FINALS

Manchester United v Arsenal

For the second season running, Arsenal faced English opposition in the latter stages of the Champions League. Last season it was Liverpool in the quarter-finals, this time it was Manchester United in the semis. The Gunners lost 1-0 but in truth that scoreline flattered the visitors. Had goalkeeper Manuel Almunia not been in such inspired form, United would surely have added to John O'Shea's 16th minute goal. Adebayor came closest to netting for the visitors but his shot went over the bar. Arsenal would need to be better in the second-leg at Emirates Stadium.

Euro fact: This was the two clubs' first ever meeting in European competition.

Arsenal v Manchester United

The Club placed flags on all the seats at Emirates in the hope of creating a colourful, inspiring atmosphere for the players as they faced the task of overcoming the deficit and reaching the second final. However, within 11 minutes the visitors had scored through Ji-Sung Park and Cristiano Ronaldo. Try as Arsenal did to get back in the game, the next goal was scored by Ronaldo, putting the tie beyond the reach of Wenger's team. Van Persie netted from the spot on 75 minutes but that was mere – and scant – consolation.

Euro fact: This match concluded the Club's second best ever Champions League campaign.

29 April 2009 Manchester United 1-0 Arsenal

5 May 2009 Arsenal 1-3 Manchester United (Van Persie 75 pen)

5 GREAT CHAMPIONS

Arsenal have starred in the UEFA Champions League under Arsène Wenger's expert guidance. During some memorable performances there have been some magnificent goals. Here are five of the best, so sit back and enjoy some goal-den memories...

1) Cesc Fabregas v Juventus

Patrick Vieira's return to Highbury was ruined by a goal from the young man who replaced him – Cesc Fabregas. "It's the young pretender," screamed the television commentator when the Spaniard netted this goal. Robert Pires successfully tackled Vieira on the halfway line, surged forward with the ball at his feet and passed to Henry. The captain then threaded the ball to Fabregas who slotted home to the delight of the home crowd.

2) Thierry Henry v Real Madrid

Two minutes into the second-half with the scoreline goalless, Henry received the ball from Fabregas in the centre-circle. With the wind in his sails he raced towards the goal, leaving opponents trailing helplessly in his wake. On reaching the penalty box he was at a difficult angle but coolly shot what proved to be the winning goal of not just the night but the tie. Some had predicted that the Gunners would come unstuck against the Spanish giants, but thanks to the captain's goal it was Real who left the competition at this stage.

3) Emmanuel Adebayor v Liverpool

Although the Togan administered the neat finishing touch, this is a goal that is remembered more for the contribution of Theo Walcott. The young Englishman picked up the ball some 80 yards from goal. He then proceeded to run towards the goal. Numerous Liverpool players attempted to check his run but none of their interventions were successful. On and on he ran, in unstoppable form. As he reached the penalty area he delivered a neat cross to Adebayor who slotted home.

4) Cesc Fabregas v Milan

The scoreline was blank until six minutes from the end of the second-leg of this knockout tie – then the Spaniard intervened. He had come close to scoring in the first-half, but his effort bounced off the bar. In the 84th minute he made no mistake. Shooting from 30 yards out, he watched his low effort sail past the despairing dive of Zeljko Kalac. The travelling fans celebrated wildly and so did the players, with the scorer celebrating by sliding to his knees in front of the bench.

5) Sol Campbell v Barcelona

After just 18 minutes of the Final in Paris, Arsenal were reduced to 10 men after the dismissal of Jens Lehmann. Their chances of going ahead in the Final seemed slim – but nobody told Sol Campbell that. In the 37th minute, the Gunners won a free-kick outside the penalty area. Henry floated the ball into the area and Campbell eluded his marker Oleguer to head home the opener. The defender was to leave Arsenal in the summer, his final contribution had been to score in the Final of the UEFA Champions League – not bad at all!

SEASON IN QUOTES

We remember football seasons in many different ways – the brilliant games, the great goals and memorable moments. Now you can relive the season by what your favourite Gunners had to say about events during 2008/09...

"I could not dream of a better start, to score in my first game after four minutes. Now I will have to continue week in and week out, and hopefully I can keep playing like this. That will be brilliant."
Samir Nasri on his goal scoring debut against West Bromwich Albion on the opening day of the season.

"I'm not scared of saying that he is the key player in the squad."
Gael Clichy approves of Fabregas being handed the captaincy.

"He's so calm in front of goal and that always gives you a smile. He's never in any stress."
Arsène Wenger on Mexican Carlos Vela's hat-trick in the 6-0 demolition of Sheffield United in the Carling Cup.

"It was a crazy game. There were so many chances it seemed like a training match."
Manuel Almunia on the 5-2 Champions League win over Fenerbahce in October.

"I would like to keep the positives tonight because I believe we were really outstanding and I don't believe that the lack of maturity is linked to experience."
The manager on the spectacular 4-4 draw with Tottenham Hotspur.

"It is a strange situation because we have created the same amount of chances as we did tonight in many games but didn't win."
The manager on ending the goal drought against West Bromwich Albion in March.

"The longer I stay the more difficult it becomes to envisage leaving."
Arsène Wenger on his bind with Arsenal Football Club.

"There is a talent at Arsenal. The difference is that they are growing up together."
Senior player Mikael Silvestre on his younger team-mates.

"I've been glued to the goals. I watched them sometimes even when I did not want to watch them because I have seen them so much on television."
Arsène Wenger on Andrey Arshavin's four goals at Anfield in April.

"I feel we are unbeatable. I go out there thinking we can win every game."
Robin van Persie on renewed optimism in March.

"My heart was nearly out. I'm sorry I couldn't have saved more than one. In the end it was enough and I am so happy to go through to the next round."
Manuel Almunia after the penalty shoot-out triumph over Roma.

"Since I was young I've always said there are no pink boots and the day they come I want to play in them."
Nicklas Bendtner on his colourful footwear.

"We have to do the dirty work, like we have learned from this year, and take that into next season."
Theo Walcott on the lessons learned from the campaign.

"I think Tony Colbert has spent more time with Eduardo than with his wife. So perhaps he deserves that kind of hug."
Wenger on the returning Eduardo's goal celebration with fitness coach Colbert.

SEASON REPORT
FA CUP

The Gunners were in fine form during an impressive campaign in the famous old competition. They came within a whisker of making the final and gave much cause for cheer along the way...

3RD ROUND

Home v Plymouth Argyle

In his first game as Arsenal captain, Dutchman Robin van Persie struck twice to help the Gunners to a comfortable 3-1 victory. He opened the scoring with a header shortly before the break and concluded the scoring just six minutes before the final whistle. In between, Bendtner had bundled a goal and Karl Duguid had struck a consolation effort for the visitors. No cup shocks here, though: the Gunners were in the Fourth Round and looking very good.

Match fact: Van Persie's opener was the 150th Arsenal goal scored at Emirates Stadium.

Arsenal

4TH ROUND

Away v Cardiff City
It proved to be a tough trip to Wales for Wenger's wonder boys. For the first half hour they were under pressure from the hosts but in the final 60 minutes, the Gunners managed to exert more of a grip on the game. Even then, though, they were unable to open the scoring. Van Persie, the hero of the previous round, came closest to doing so with a swivelling shot midway through the second half. The game ended goalless and a replay at Emirates was booked.

Match fact: This was midfielder Aaron Ramsay's first return to his former club.

REPLAY

Home v Cardiff City
Exactly 358 days previous to this tie, Eduardo was stretchered from the field at Birmingham City with a fractured leg and a dislocated ankle. This was his comeback match for the first-team and by the time he was substituted on 67 minutes he had already scored two goals, one from the penalty spot. He was joined on the scoresheet by Third Round scorers Bendtner and Van Persie as the Gunners soared into the Fifth Round. It had been an inspirational evening thanks to Eduardo's happy return.

Match fact: Midfielder Denilson celebrated his 21st birthday on this day.

5TH ROUND

Home v Burnley

The Gunners soared into the quarter-finals with beautiful strikes from Vela and Eduardo. Then, six minutes from time, Eboue sealed the win by adding a third. It was a positive afternoon in general, with Walcott returning from a four-month absence due to injury. Eduardo captained the team and it was his strike that was the pick of the bunch. Song sent a tempting cross to the far post where the Croatian eluded his marker and then fired the ball home cheekily with the outside of his boot. It was a strike that fans dream of scoring, and at the end of the tie the Gunners faithful were daring to dream of Wembley.

Match fact: This was Arsenal's 17th game without defeat.

Home v Hull City

The Gunners began this game going behind to a strike from former Tottenham Hotspur star Nick Barmby and ended it with a place in the FA Cup semi-final for the 26th time in the Club's illustrious history. The Arsenal goals came late in the second-half. In the 74th minute, Arshavin set up Van Persie to level the scoreline. Then 10 minutes later Gallas nodded the winner. Chelsea awaited in the semi-finals.

Match fact: The Gunners had gone four months unbeaten in domestic competition going into this tie.

SEMI-FINAL

Arsenal v Chelsea

The Gunners were back at Wembley and the game started well for Wenger's team. After 18 minutes, Walcott fired Arsenal ahead with a fine strike. The young striker had also opened the scoring when the two sides met in the Carling Cup Final two years previously, but Arsenal ultimately lost that tie thanks to a late winner from Didier Drogba. Lightning struck twice when the same man was responsible for the finishing touch to Chelsea's victory, netting the winner six minutes from time after Florent Malouda had equalised in the first-half. It was a heartbreaking end to a fine FA Cup campaign from Arsenal.

RESULTS

Third Round 3 January 2009 Arsenal 3-1 Plymouth Argyle (Van Persie 47, 84, Bendtner 49)

Fourth Round 25 January 2009 Cardiff City 0-0 Arsenal

Fourth Round (replay) 16 February 2009 Arsenal 4-0 Cardiff City (Eduardo 20, 60, Bendtner 39, Van Persie 74)

Fifth Round 8 March 2009 Arsenal 3-0 Burnley (Vela 24, Eduardo 51, Eboue 84)

Fifth Round 17 March 2009, Arsenal 2-1 Hull City (Van Persie 74, Gallas 84)

Semi-finals 18 April 2009 Chelsea 2-1 Arsenal (Walcott 18)

EMIRATES STADIUM

With the Club approaching its fourth year at Emirates Stadium, it is now a familiar place for all Gunners fans and truly feels like home. However, how well do you know the Club's headquarters? By the time you have read this collection of essential and non-essential Emirates facts you will be head of the class...

The Emirates Stadium was officially opened by HRH Duke of Edinburgh, Prince Philip, on Thursday 26 October 2006.

There are 100 flights of stairs, their combined height is enough to go to the top of Canary Wharf twice over! There are also 13 elevators and five banks of escalators.

The pitch is 113m by 76m.

The first eight Premier League matches at Emirates Stadium ended either 3-0 or 1-1.

Theo Walcott provided the first assist for the first goal at the stadium which was scored by Gilberto against Aston Villa on 19 August 2006.

Crutches are allowed into the stadium and should be placed safely under your seat.

The ITV reality pop show The X Factor has held auditions at Emirates Stadium, which is where winner Alexandra Burke auditioned!

Emmanuel Adebayor scored the stadium's first goal against Tottenham Hotspur.

The stadium has a cycle park which can hold up to 150 bicycles.

The Gunners' biggest win at the stadium was the 6-0 victory over Sheffield United in the Carling Cup in September 2008.

It is the third biggest football stadium in England.

The stadium's first international match was a friendly between Argentina and Brazil, in September 2006. Brazil won 3-0.

Bruce Springsteen performed the first rock concert at the stadium.

In March 2008, British Prime Minister Gordon Brown and French President Nicolas Sarkozy held a summit at the stadium.

There are approximately 250 catering points. Yum!

The highest-scoring tie at the stadium was the 4-4 draw with Tottenham Hotspur in October 2008.

The 3-0 win against Newcastle in August 2008 was also the first time Arsenal kept four successive Premier League clean sheets at Emirates Stadium.

Emmanuel Adebayor scored the first hat-trick at the stadium against Derby County in September 2007...

...and a year and a day later Carlos Vela netted the second, against Sheffield United.

The Gunners have fared well in Europe at the Emirates. When Arsenal lost to Manchester United in the UEFA Champions League semi-final second leg in May 2009, it brought to an end a 17-match unbeaten home run in the competition.

The first game at Emirates Stadium was a 1-1 draw against Aston Villa. The 50th game saw the same opponents and the same scoreline.

The 9,000 Plymouth Argyle fans who travelled to watch their team take on Arsenal in the FA Cup third round in January 2009 formed the biggest away following to a game at the Emirates.

As is now customary, Arsène Wenger sent out young sides to compete in the competition – and once more they did him proud. Here is the story of their 2008/09 Carling Cup heroics.

Arsenal v Sheffield United
A hat-trick from a Mexican, two goals from a Dane and one from a young Englishman – it was a memorable evening of football against The Blades. It was Bendtner who got the rout underway, curling a shot home on the half hour and doubling the lead three minutes before half-time. Carlos Vela then scored either side of the interval and completed his hat-trick when he converted a fine pass from Aaron Ramsey. By this time, 16-year-old Jack Wilshere had broken his duck with a fine low shot at the near post.

Arsenal v Wigan Athletic

The Gunners were on similarly outstanding form against Wigan in the next round. This time, young Jay Simpson celebrated his first start for the Club by scoring two fine goals. His first came after 43 minutes, before which he had already showed his threat by rattling a shot against the crossbar. When he ran onto a through ball by Jack Wilshere in the 68th minute he made no mistake with his shot and added a second. Five minutes later the impressive Vela completed the scoring with a cute chip over the advancing Chris Kirkland. The Gunners were in the last eight of the competition!

Burnley v Arsenal

It was 'just one of those nights' for the young Gunners at Turf Moor where a combination of fine goalkeeping and plain bad luck consigned them to a 2-0 defeat and an exit from the competition. Bendtner, Randall and Vela were all denied goals thanks to the brilliance on the night of Brian Jensen in the opposition goal. Meanwhile, Fran Merida was unable to match a glorious run with a clinical finish and saw his shot trickle wide of the post. It was a freezing night in Burnley and the travelling fans were not warmed by the two goals from Kevin McDonald which sent them home empty-handed. That said, the young Gunners had shown their class during the Carling Cup campaign and pointed to a bright future for them and their supporters.

23 September 2008 Arsenal 6-0 Sheffield United
(Bendtner 31, 42, Vela 44, 49, 86, Wilshere 57)

11 November 2008 Arsenal 3-0 Wigan Athletic
(Simpson 42, 66, Vela 70)

2 December 2008 Burnley 2-0 Arsenal

50 FANTASTIC FACTS
ANDREY ARSHAVIN

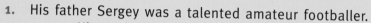

He is the new hotshot Gunner, but how much do you know about Andrey Arshavin? Read your way through these 50 facts and you will be an expert on the boy from Russia...

1. His father Sergey was a talented amateur footballer.
2. His star sign is Gemini.
3. He was born on May 29 1981.
4. He was born in St. Petersburg, which was then known as Leningrad.
5. He was hit by a car as a child: "it sent me 10 metres into the air," he recalls.
6. As a boy he supported Barcelona.
7. He used to milk cows and gather mushrooms at his grandparents' farm.
8. He had to be held down by four doctors when he needed a tooth removed.
9. He was good at maths and chemistry at school.
10. He has a diploma in fashion.
11. He is an accomplished draughts player.
12. He won the League Cup with Zenit in 2003.
13. Zenit play their home games at the Petrovsky Stadium.
14. He was runner-up in the Russian Footballer of the Year list in 2001, 2002 and 2004.
15. In 2004, he was named Best Second Striker in the Russian Premier League by sports newspaper "Sport-Express", and voted the country's best player by readers of newspaper "Soviet Sport".
16. He was the 2006 Russian Footballer of the Year.
17. The same year, he was voted "Best Footballer" by three leading sport journals in Russia - the weekly "Football" and the newspapers "Sport-Express" and "Soviet Sport".
18. He started his career as a right-sided midfielder.
19. He made his debut for Zenit in the Intertoto Cup at Bradford City in 2000. The visitors won 2-0.
20. He made his international debut for Russia against Belarus on May 17, 2002.
21. He scored his first international goal against Romania on February 13 2003.

22. He has written a thesis on the development of the sportswear production process.

23. He was made captain of Zenit in 2007.

24. The same year he won the Russian Premier League with Zenit.

25. Arsène Wenger described him as "the revelation of the Euro 2008".

26. He was the top assist-maker in the club's triumphant 2007/08 UEFA Cup.

27. The same year, he also won the European Super Cup and Russian Super Cup with Zenit.

28. He made 232 appearances for Zenit, and scored 51 goals.

29. In October 2008, Arshavin was nominated for the prestigious Ballon d'Or award (European Footballer of the Year award).

30. He signed for Arsenal with just an hour left of the January 2009 transfer window.

31. He made his Arsenal debut against Sunderland on February 21 2009.

32. He almost scored twice in that game.

33. He scored his first Arsenal goal against Blackburn Rovers on March 15 2009.

34. Arsenal's Under-18s striker Sanchez Watt spotted a coach's streak in the Russian during a pre-season game against Barnet. "Arshavin taught me a lot about my positioning," he enthused.

35. He has a recurring dream of being a horse in a field surrounded by guinea pigs.

36. His girlfriend said she struggled with English cuisine: "For a person used to Russian cuisine, it's difficult to instantly accept another kind. I was brought up on my granny's piroshki (Russian pie) and my mother's soup".

37. He plays the Football Manager game on his PC.

38. He played 997 minutes for Arsenal in Season 2008/09.

39. He offered funding to the Smyena football academy.

40. He was Arsenal.com Player of the Month in April and May 2009.

41. Wenger says of him: "He is not a soft boy at all".

42. On joining the Club he took the number 23 shirt, previously worn by Sol Campbell. The number was made famous by basketball legend Michael Jordan.

43. He was part of the Team of the Tournament for Euro 2008.

44. He scored four times at Liverpool in April 2009, becoming only the 10th Gunner to score four times in one match away from home.

45. After he arrived in English football he said he was "surprised" by how competitive the game here is.

46. He began to learn the English language in 2007.

47. He has scored in every competition that the Russian national team has competed it.

48. He is five foot eight inches tall.

49. In 2007, the Daily Telegraph newspaper dubbed him "Russia's artful dodger".

50. He likes singing karaoke.

January 1 – Jack Wilshere's birthday (born 1992).

January 16 – Nicklas Bendtner's birthday (born 1988).

January 19 – Legendary Club manager Herbert Chapman was born in 1878.

February 11 – The Club left its first home (Plumstead Common) and moved to the Manor Ground in 1888.

February 14 – Bacary Sagna's birthday (born 1983).

February 25 – Eduardo's birthday (born 1983).

March 12 – Arsenal recorded their biggest ever victory, 12-0 against Loughborough Town in 1900.

March 30 – Arsenal play Manchester United (then known as Newton Heath) for the first time, winning 3-2 in 1895.

April 3 – 'Woolwich' was officially dropped from the Club's name in 1914.

April 25 – The Gunners win the Premiership at White Hart Lane, en route to an unbeaten league season (2004).

May 4 – Cesc Fabregas's birthday (born 1987).

May 6 – Arsenal's record north London derby win, beating Spurs 6-0 at White Hart Lane in 1935.

May 8 – Arsenal won the second part of the Premiership and FA Cup double thanks to a 1-0 win at Old Trafford in 2002.

May 16 – Arsenal beat Newcastle United 2-0 in the FA Cup Final to claim their first double under Arsène Wenger (1998).

May 19 – Manuel Almunia's birthday (born 1977).

May 26 – The Gunners win the league thanks to a last minute goal at Anfield from Michael Thomas in 1989.

June 11 – Legendary Midfielder Liam Brady joined the Gunners as an apprentice in 1971.

Want to brush up on important anniversaries in Arsenal Football Club's prestigious history? Keen to know when your favourite Gunners' birthday is? Then keep this calendar of significant Club dates handy and you won't go far wrong...

June 14 – Manager Arsène Wenger received an honorary OBE in 2003.

July 1 – Future Arsenal captain Cesc Fabregas signs for the Club in 2003.

July 26 – Gael Clichy's birthday (born 1985).

July 30 – England won the World Cup in 1966 with a team including future Gunner Alan Ball.

August 3 – Future Club skipper Thierry Henry signed for the Club from Juventus in 1999.

August 6 – Robin van Persie's birthday (born 1983).

September 1 – Arsenal recorded their biggest ever win over Liverpool, 8-1 at Highbury in 1934.

September 9 – Alex Song's birthday (born 1987).

September 13 – Ian Wright became the Club's then leading goalscorer with three goals against Bolton Wanderers in 1997.

October 12 – Arsène Wenger took charge for his first game, a 2-0 away win at Blackburn Rovers in 1996.

October 22 – Arsène Wenger's birthday (born 1949).

November 5 – The Gillespie Road tube station officially changes its name to Arsenal, at the request of Manager Herbert Chapman in 1932.

November 29 – Arsenal recorded their biggest ever win at Stamford Bridge, beating Chelsea 5-1 in 1930.

December 14 – Ted Drake scored all seven of Arsenal's goals in the 7-1 thrashing of Aston Villa in 1935.

December 26 – Aaron Ramsey's birthday (born 1990).

Okay, so you're an Arsenal supporter but how red is the blood that flows through your veins? Are you a fair-weather fan or a football fanatic? Here are 20 signs that you are an Arsenal superfan...

Your bedroom is painted red and white.

You sleep in your Arsenal kit.

Your dog is called Cesc and your cat is called Theo.

When your Dad bought a new van you asked him to call it 'Persie'.

When you sneeze during the week, your first thought is: 'I can't be ill, I can't miss the match on Saturday!'

You have already put your future kids down for a season ticket and decided that they will be called 'Arsenal'.

You are on first name terms with individual blades of grass at Emirates Stadium.

Your voice is hoarse every Monday morning because you were cheering on the Gunners at the weekend.

When you are doing sums in maths class the numbers make you think of the shirt numbers of players (Cesc Fabregas + William Gallas = 11).

You can remember and re-enact each players' favourite goal celebration.

When you go on holiday in the summer you know instantly which Arsenal players were born in the country you visit.

Your parents have to pay you to stop talking about Arsenal during long car journeys.

When Arsenal win a match, friends congratulate you as if you were responsible.

If there was a fire in your home the first thing you would save would be your Arsenal shirt.

You always play as Arsenal on computer games.

You have re-watched games on television so many times that you can recite the commentary off by heart.

Your favourite food is... whatever you eat at Emirates Stadium.

You celebrate your favourite players' birthday just as passionately as your own.

When a young player makes his debut for the Club, you already know all about him before he even sets foot on the pitch.

You play for Arsenal on the hallowed turf of Emirates Stadium...... every night..........in your dreams.

ARSENAL SOCCER SCHOOLS

Arsenal Soccer Schools have been operating for more than 20 years both in the UK and internationally. As manager Arsène Wenger says: "Our soccer school courses welcome children of all abilities and it doesn't matter which team children support, we just want everyone to have fun whilst learning to play football the Arsenal way!"

Europe

* There are two Arsenal Soccer Schools in Ireland – they are in Dublin and County Meath.
* There are a total of 17 Arsenal Soccer Schools in the UK as far apart as Cornwall and Lincolnshire.
* The Netherlands branch is based near Rotterdam.
* In Midi-Pyrenees there is the French Arsenal Soccer School.
* There are also branches in Spain, Italy and Greece.

Asia

* There are branches in Oman, Dubai and Bahrain.
* Thailand and Vietnam are home to Arsenal Soccer School outposts.
* There are also Schools in Vietnam, Singapore and Indonesia.

North America & Canada

* Durham Indoor Soccer Center in Canada has been operating Arsenal Soccer Schools since 2002.
* The first Arsenal Soccer Schools in America were launched in the summer of 2009 in Colarado, Massachusetts and Georgia.
* The Hawaiian Arsenal Soccer School was announced in May 2009.

Africa

* The Wadi Degla Club in Egypt runs an Arsenal Soccer School.

Oceania

* Football Pathways operates an Arsenal Soccer School in Queensland, Australia.
* The other branch is in New South Wales.

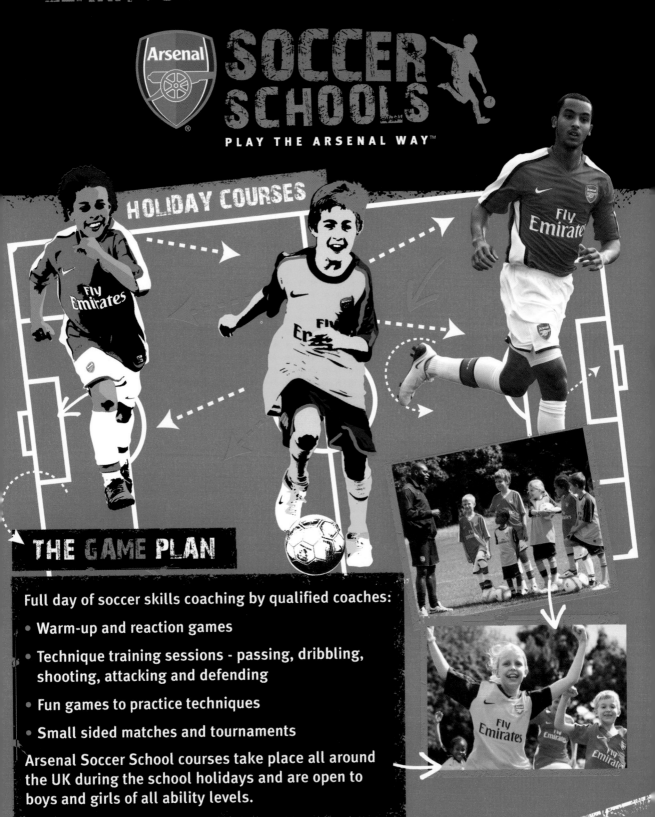

TAKE YOUR GAME TO THE NEXT LEVEL
LEARN TO PLAY THE ARSENAL WAY!

Arsenal SOCCER SCHOOLS
PLAY THE ARSENAL WAY™

HOLIDAY COURSES

THE GAME PLAN

Full day of soccer skills coaching by qualified coaches:

- Warm-up and reaction games
- Technique training sessions - passing, dribbling, shooting, attacking and defending
- Fun games to practice techniques
- Small sided matches and tournaments

Arsenal Soccer School courses take place all around the UK during the school holidays and are open to boys and girls of all ability levels.

45

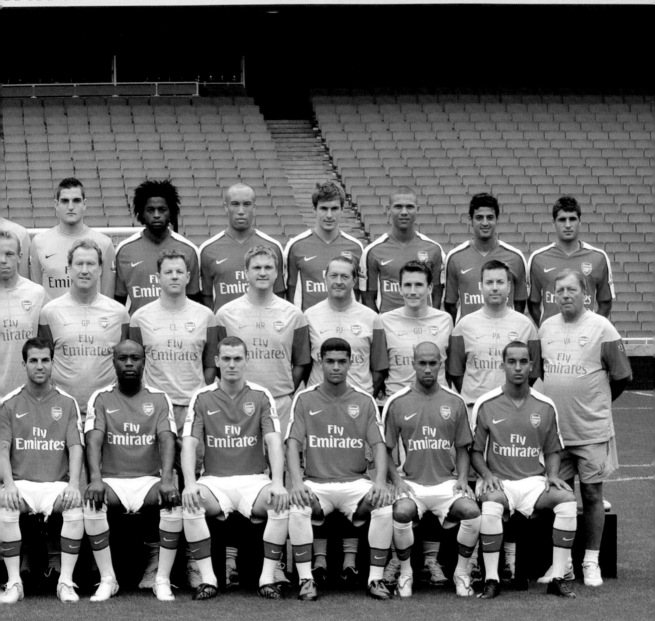

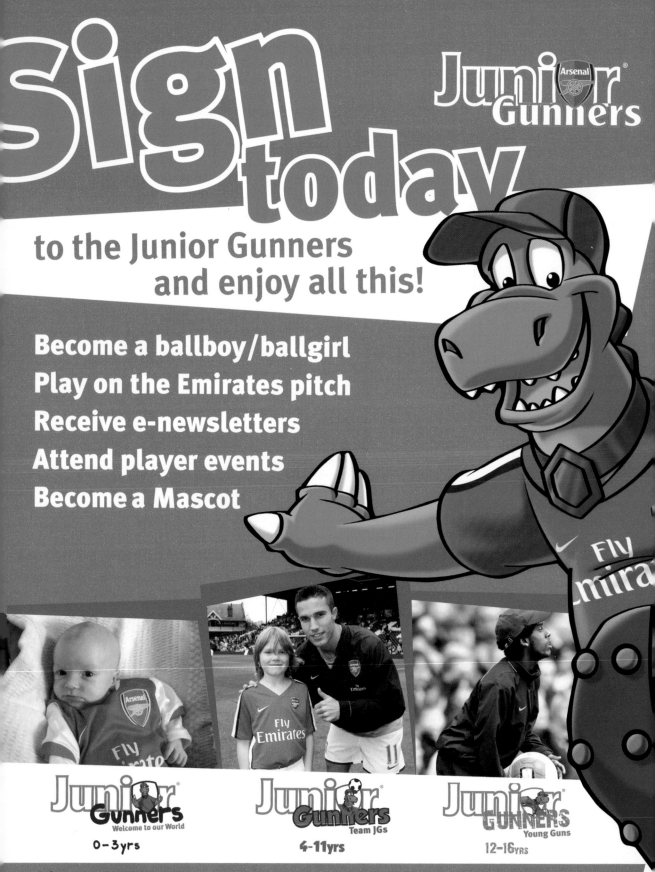

junior GUNNERS

Exciting news: after listening to feedback from Junior Gunners members and their parents the Club has decided to split JG membership into three age groups. The new look membership offers JGs exciting new packs along with all of the benefits they have come to expect from the Club!

Welcome to our World (0-3 year-olds)

For boys and girls from birth to three years of age this is the best way to begin your involvement with the Club. Members will receive:

* A fantastic Welcome to our World membership pack, featuring a mini Gunnersaurus, beaker, cool bag with lunch box and a Gunnersaurus height chart
* Birthday card and Arsenal shopping voucher
* A chance to attend a Welcome to our World event with Ambassador Robin van Persie
* Member updates via the bespoke Junior Gunners website and e-newsletters

Team JGs (4-11 year-olds)

Team JGs is part of the official membership scheme for boys and girls from four years of age to 11 years of age with the following benefits:

* A fantastic membership pack including a Team JGs shoulder bag, set of training cones, mini football and drink bottle
* The chance to be selected as a first team mascot
* Exclusive newsletter sent twice a year
* Access to reduced price tickets (subject to availability)
* Competitions and exclusive events, one of which is attended by Ambassador Emmanuel Eboue
* Priority notice for Soccer Schools courses
* The chance to be nominated for a Junior Gunner Award
* Member updates via the bespoke Junior Gunners website and e-newsletters

Young Guns (12-16 year-olds)

For boys and girls aged 12-16 (16 years or younger on 31st August 2009) Young Guns offers members loads of great benefits:

* A souvenir pack including a Young Guns wash bag, beanie hat, passport holder, and Arsenal year book
* The chance to be selected as a first team mascot
* Exclusive newsletter sent twice a year
* Access to reduced price tickets (subject to availability)
* Competitions and exclusive events, one of which is attended by Ambassador Manuel Almunia
* Priority notice for Soccer Schools courses
* The chance to be nominated for a Junior Gunner Award
* Member updates via the bespoke Junior Gunners website and e-newsletters

DOING THE MATH!

1 Appearance by Vito Mannone.

3 Goals scored by Carlos Vela against Sheffield United in the Carling Cup.

4 Goals scored by Andrey Arshavin in one match against Liverpool.

6 Premier League games lost.

8 Goals in one game against both Tottenham Hotspur and Liverpool.

9 Teenagers in the starting-line up against Burnley in the Carling Cup quarter-final.

10 Premier League assists by Cesc Fabregas.

11 Goals scored in the UEFA Champions League group stage.

12 Premier League games drawn.

20 Premier League games won.

21 Points ahead of Tottenham Hotspur in the final Premier League standings.

24 Substitute appearances by Nicklas Bendtner.

31 Premier League goal difference.

32 Number of games unbeaten that Arsenal had gone before losing to Hull City in September.

38 Premier League games played.

63 Hours between the Champions League tie against Porto and the Premier League meeting with Middlesbrough in December.

68 Premier League goals scored.

69 Premier League games it took Emmanuel Eboue to score his first league goal for the Club.

The 2008/09 season in numbers...

72 Premier League points.

163 Passes completed by Bacary Sagna (Premier League).

195 Minutes per goal from Nicklas Bendtner (Premier League).

364 The minutes Arsenal went without a goal in February.

997 Minutes played by Andrey Arshavin (Premier League).

1,091 Minutes played by Mikael Silvestre (Premier League).

1,900 Minutes played by Cesc Fabregas (Premier League).

2,868 Minutes played by Manuel Almunia (Premier League).

6,931 Minutes between the first and 150th goals at Emirates Stadium.

9,000 Number of Plymouth Argyle fans who travelled to Emirates for the FA Cup Third Round tie in January.

60,082 Attendance for the home tie with Stoke.

STAT ATTACK!

Top goalscorer: Robin van Persie (20)
Most appearances: Denilson (49)

League Table

		P	W	D	L	F	A	+/-	Pts
1	Manchester United	38	28	6	4	68	24	44	90
2	Liverpool	38	25	11	2	77	27	50	86
3	Chelsea	38	25	8	5	68	24	44	83
4	Arsenal	38	20	12	6	68	37	31	72

YOUNG GUNS!

Arsenal's first-team squad has plenty of incredible young talents in its number. However, sniffing at their heels for a first-team place is an army of even younger football aces who are poised to become the next set of Arsenal stars. Here are some of the best...

Name: Kieran Gibbs
Position: Defender   Born: 26 September 1989

Defensive ace Gibbs joined Arsenal in September 2007 from Wimbledon. He made his debut the following month in the 3-0 victory over Sheffield United in the Carling Cup. The Lambeth-born lad has since enjoyed a successful loan spell at Norwich City before returning to north London where he has gone from strength to strength. Appearing in all domestic competitions and the UEFA Champions League, he has drawn complimentary observations from numerous witnesses, including legendary Arsenal left-back Nigel Winterburn, who won several league titles with the Club in the 1980s and 1990s. Gibbs would love to emulate that success!

Name: Gavin Hoyte
Position: Defender   Born: 6 June 1990

Having been at the Club since the age of nine, Hoyte is Arsenal through and through. The younger brother of Gunners star Justin Hoyte, he is athletic and pacey just like his sibling. He has played in all defensive positions and impressed in each, particularly at centre-back. He has great leadership skills and has captained the reserve side. One of the fastest players in the country, he has also excelled at international level where he has turned out for the England Under-19s. Watch out for him, he will be outpacing many an opponent at a stadium near you soon!

Name: Jack Wilshere
Position: Midfielder   **Born: 1 January 1992**
Wilshere joined the Club as a nine year old in 2001. In February 2008, the Hertfordshire-born midfielder made his first Reserve Team appearance against West Ham United – he was still a schoolboy. Just seven months later, he made his debut for the senior side aged just 16 years and 256 days. He says he has received lots of advice from his manager and team-mates – one in particular. "They all talk to me and tell me what it was like for them when they were young players," he said. "But Theo Walcott is the one who helped me especially in that area."

Name: Mark Randall
Position: Midfielder   **Born: 28 September 1989**
Randall made his first-team debut against West Bromwich Albion in the Carling Cup in 2006. The Gunners won that tie 2-0. He subsequently gained extra experience during a loan spell at Burnley. In 2007/08 he appeared in both the quarter-final and semi-final of the Carling Cup, as he showed increasing talent and maturity. He then made his Premier League debut against Sunderland in May 2008. A creative and composed talent, he has since appeared in all domestic competitions and the Club has high hopes for him for the future.

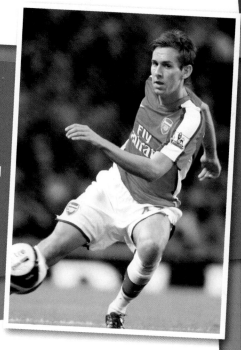

Name: Luke Freeman
Position: Striker   **Born: 22 March 1992**
Former Gillingham youngster Freeman signed professional forms for Arsenal in April 2009. He had made his debut for the Kent side at the highly tender age of 15 years and 233 days, which made him not just the Club's youngest player but also the youngest FA Cup participant. He scored seven goals in 15 appearances for Steve Bould's Under-18s in 2008/09. The young forward also made one substitute appearance for the Reserves. Young Freeman has all the makings of a fine forward at first-team level.

Arsenal

GAEL CLICHY

SAMIR NASRI

TRIVIA QUIZ

The Back Line

1. Which country was Manuel Almunia born in?
2. Which club did Bacary Sagna join the Gunners from: Auxerre or Aston Villa?
3. Mikael Silvestre won the treble with Manchester United in which year?
4. Which London club did William Gallas join the Gunners from?
5. How many Premier League goals did Arsenal concede in 2008/09?
6. What nationality is Gael Clichy?
7. Kolo Toure made his Arsenal debut in the Community Shield in which year: 2002 or 1997?
8. What year was Mikael Silvestre born: 1977 or 1987?
9. What is the surname of Arsenal's Polish goalkeeper Lukasz?
10. Which former defensive Arsenal star now coaches the Gunners youth team?

Middle Class

1. Which Spanish Arsenal midfielder scored his first Gunners goal against Wolves in December 2003?
2. How old was Jack Wilshere when he made his Arsenal debut?
3. Which Turkish side did Aaron Ramsey score his first Champions League goal against?
4. How many goals did Andrey Arshavin score against Liverpool in April 2009?
5. Which former Arsenal captain has Abou Diaby been compared with by Arsène Wenger?
6. What nationality is Samir Nasri?
7. And which club did he score his first Premier League goal against?
8. Which young Arsenal midfielder once played for Sao Paulo?
9. Emmanuel Eboue scored twice against which Premier League side in March 2009?
10. What is the nationality of Tomas Rosicky?

Striking Gold!

1. Which team did Theo Walcott join Arsenal from?
2. Is Robin van Persie Dutch or German?
3. Celta Vigo is the club that which striker joined Arsenal from?
4. Nicklas Bendtner scored twice against which team in May 2009?
5. What nationality is Carlos Vela?
6. Eduardo's career-threatening injury came during a match with which opponents: Barnet or Birmingham City?
7. Robin van Persie first captained Arsenal against Plymouth Argyle in 2008/09: true or false?
8. How many Premier League goals did Arsenal score in total in 2008/09?
9. Which Gunner scored during the FA Cup semi-final with Chelsea?
10. Who is Arsenal's all-time record goalscorer?

History Lesson

1. Arsenal won their first double under Arsène Wenger in which year?
2. And in which year did they win their second Wenger double?
3. In which year did the Club win its first FA Cup: 1930 or 1903?
4. The Gunners won the European Cup Winners Cup in 1993 against which Italian side: Parma or AC Milan?
5. What year was the Club founded in?
6. Who was Arsenal manager before Arsène Wenger: Bruce Rioch or Herbert Chapman?
7. Which Frenchman is the leading goalscorer of all-time for Arsenal?
8. The Gunners beat the same Sheffield side in both the FA Cup Final and League Cup Final of 1993. Was it United or Wednesday?
9. Which season did Arsenal win the Premier League without losing a single league game?
10. In which year did Arsenal move to the Emirates Stadium?

The Manager

1. What country was Mr Wenger managing in before he joined Arsenal?
2. And with which team?
3. Which team were the first opponents of his Arsenal career?
4. And in which year?
5. In which year did he win his first FA Cup?
6. And against which opposition?
7. He has an OBE. True or false?
8. What year was Mr Wenger born in: 1949 or 1959?
9. He won the French championship with Marseille. True or false?
10. How many doubles has Wenger won with Arsenal?

Answers page 61.

CROSSWORD

Across
1. The first name of Silvestre (6)
3. The Club mascot is called _____ (12)
4. Our Brazilian midfield ace? (8)
6. Which London team did Arsenal draw 4-4 with in 2008/09? (9)
8. What football is all about (5)
10. A goal scored from the top of the body (6)
13. The Club's home is _____ Stadium (8)
14. Our brilliant manager, Mr _____ (6)
17. The Club's former home (8)
18. Arsenal scored five in one match against which Turkish side? (10)

Down
2. And against which team did Arshavin score four goals in the same season? (9)
3. What is Manuel Almunia's position? (10)
5. The surname of the brilliant Cesc? (8)
7. Arsenal's opponents in the FA Cup semi-final (7)
9. Strikers love to _____ a goal (5)
11. Arsenal won this in 2004 (11)
12. The nationality of Clichy and Nasri (6)
15. How many points are awarded for a league win? (5)
16. The Club's home colours are red and ____ (5)

Answer page 61.

WORD SEARCH

Can you find the names of the following 10 Arsenal players of recent years that are hidden in this wordsearch grid? You will need eagle-eyes to do it – good luck Gunners fans!

V	H	A	P	V	A	R	B	J	E	C	O	F	B	O
H	A	K	J	S	I	E	Z	M	W	B	N	V	V	J
E	H	D	U	K	O	E	D	W	X	U	O	V	B	X
K	P	E	G	H	R	N	A	R	G	G	C	U	I	O
V	I	C	N	G	O	Z	G	N	R	I	E	E	E	T
E	R	F	S	R	L	T	L	T	I	R	U	J	Q	D
L	E	Q	T	B	Y	M	K	O	W	N	S	F	S	R
A	S	N	Y	C	H	T	B	U	J	N	A	X	H	V
W	J	C	T	G	S	X	S	R	X	S	M	S	C	P
S	C	L	I	C	H	Y	A	E	Q	A	E	Q	R	J
R	Z	Q	M	R	U	C	Q	O	L	G	L	R	R	I
I	U	A	I	A	W	T	U	P	T	N	S	X	U	R
X	W	C	E	S	C	Y	K	Z	J	A	H	Y	G	V

HENRY	TOURE	NASRI	VELA	SAGNA
CLICHY	PIRES	SONG	EBOUE	CESC

Answer page 61.

TOP OF THE CHARTS!

2008/09 was a thrill-filled season for the Gunners. Can they do even better in 2009/10? Keep track of their progress here and you can compare the two campaigns!

Premier League	2008/09	2009/10
Final position	Fourth	
First home win	West Bromwich Albion 1-0	
First away win	Blackburn Rovers 4-0	
First home draw	Liverpool 1-1	
First away draw	Sunderland 1-1	
First home defeat	Hull City 2-1	
Domestic Cups		
FA Cup	Semi-final: Chelsea	
Carling Cup	Round 5: Burnley	
Champions League		
Progress	Semi-Final: Manchester United	
First home win	FC Twente 4-0	
First away win	FC Twente 2-0	
First home draw	Fenerbahce 0-0	
First away draw	Dynamo Kiev 1-1	
First home defeat	Manchester United 1-3	
First away defeat	FC Porto 0-2	
First goals in...		
Premier League	Nasri v West Bromwich Albion	
FA Cup	Van Persie v Plymouth Argyle	
Carling Cup	Bendtner v Sheffield United	

The Back Line
1. Spain
2. Auxerre
3. 1999
4. Chelsea
5. 37
6. French
7. 2002
8. 1977
9. Fabianski
10. Steve Bould

Middle Class
1. Cesc Fabregas
2. 16
3. Fenerbahce
4. 4
5. Patrick Vieira
6. French
7. West Bromwich Albion
8. Denilson
9. Blackburn Rovers
10. Czech

Striking Gold!
1. Southampton
2. Dutch
3. Carlos Vela
4. Portsmouth
5. Mexican
6. Birmingham City
7. True
8. 68
9. Theo Walcott
10. Thierry Henry

History Lesson
1. 1998
2. 2002
3. 1930
4. Parma
5. 1886
6. Bruce Rioch
7. Thierry Henry
8. Wednesday
9. 2003/04
10. 2006

The Manager
1. Japan
2. Grampus Eight Nagoya
3. Blackburn Rovers
4. 1996
5. 1998
6. Newcastle United
7. True
8. 1949
9. False, he won it with Monaco
10. Two